D1094682

Bill Reynolds

PORSCHE

The Pursuit of Excellence

Bramley Books

Bill Reynolds

PORSCHE

The Pursuit of Excellence

Featuring the photography of Nicky Wright and George Solomonides

All pictures copyright CLB Publishing except:
p69 Haymarket; p70, 71, 82, 83, 84, 85, 92, 93, 96, 97 National Motor Museum

CLB2983
This edition published 1993 by Bramley Books

Printed and bound in Hong Kong
ISBN 1-85833 051-3

The Man and the Cars

Ferdinand Anton Porsche was born on September 3, 1875 at Maffersdorf rechts der Neisse, then a part of the Austro-Hungarian Empire but today in Czechoslovakia. The first car he designed, the Porsche-Lohner Chaise, won a prize at the Paris Universal Exposition in 1900; and the very first "modern" Porsche, the 356/1, was built as a prototype almost half a century later. By the time Porsche died on January 30, 1951, he was a *Herr Professor Doktor Doktor,* and the 500th Porsche 356 was only a few weeks in the future. Today, you do not have to look too hard at a current production 911 to see the ghost of the 356. Porsche was a living history of the development of the motor vehicle, and since his death the tradition he founded has been carried on.

From the very start he was innovative. The Porsche-Lohner employed mixte drive, in which an internal combustion engine drove electric motors in the hubs of all four wheels. The logic was indisputable – clutches and gears made the internal combustion engine hard to handle, but battery-dependent electric cars had far too limited a range. Combining the two may be expensive, but it is wonderfully smooth, reliable, and simple to operate, and it is the system used in diesel-electric locomotives to this day. Lohner was also the Imperial carriage builder, and Porsche himself (who was an army reservist) drove His Imperial and Royal Highness the Archduke Ferdinand in the Porsche-Lohner, winning praise from him. In 1905, when Porsche was still only 30, he was awarded the Poetting Prize for engineering.

Porsche was not a man to rest on his laurels, though. In 1906 he was offered a seat on the board of Austro-Daimler as technical director. There, he modified various Austro-Daimler designs into racers, and in 1909 he was one of three drivers in the Austro-Daimler team which drove in the *Prinz Heinrich Fahrt,* a one-week endurance race. All three of "his" cars finished and were awarded silver plaques, but for the 1910 Prince Henry (as it was generally known) he modified the cars even more radically and his cars came in 1-2-3.

He also designed aero engines, and during the Great War he was awarded his first *Dr. Ing. h.c.* (honorary doctorate) from Vienna Technical University, and was made *Generaldirektor* of Austro-Daimler.

After the war, times were hard and he did not design a new car until 1921: the sohc Sascha, built for Count Sascha Solowrat. It won its class in the 1922 Targa Florio, but was not particularly successful thereafter. Nor was his idea of developing the engine into a low-priced "people's car" (*Volkswagen*) popular with his bosses, as they preferred to take many marks from the few, rather than a few marks each from the many. Also, Porsche had a flaming row with Austro-Daimler's bankers – who were pulling some very dubious tricks with foreign exchange, at Austro-Daimler's expense – and walked out. He was promptly hired by Daimler in Stuttgart, and there, he was responsible for the racing program.

His supercharged, 16-valve, four-cylinder single-seater was not fully developed for Indianapolis, but the following year it won the Targa Florio. This led to the Technische Hochschule in Stuttgart giving him a second honorary doctorate, and to his masters at Daimler giving him the chance to build something really new. This turned out to be a supercharged straight-eight (with four valves per cylinder), with which Rudolph Caracciola won the German Grand Prix at Avus in 1926 – the first German Grand Prix since the war.

For roadgoing use, he also designed the immortal *kompressor* Mercedes model. The original Type 600 engine was a 6.24 liter straight six designated "24/100/140," referring to the fiscal or taxation horsepower (24), the horsepower without the supercharger (100), and the horsepower with the supercharger clutched in (140). The supercharger engaged when the pedal was floored, and was intended for overtaking and for rapid acceleration to even higher cruising speed. The sound of the engine with the *kompressor* engaged has been likened to a particularly vocal pig objecting to its slaughter. As installed in the Mercedes K, it was rated at 110/160 hp, but the handling and brakes were so bad that it was popularly called the "death trap."

Within months it evolved into the Mercedes S: 6.8 liters, 120/180 hp, a new chassis and new brakes. At the Nurburgring in June 1927, Caracciola and Rosemeyer showed that this new beast had at least adequate handling: they wiped the floor with the opposition. Then followed the SS, with still more capacity and power (7022 cc and 170/225 hp, from a *magnesium* block) and the SSK for *kurz,* "short" which was a similar car but with a 116-inch (2900 mm) wheelbase instead of 134 inches (3350 mm).

At the German Grand Prix of 1928, Porsche-designed cars repeated the trick of the 1910 Prince Henry: 1-2-3. But, meanwhile, Daimler and Benz had merged, and the bean counters at Benz objected to the flashy racing program that they had inherited. On a somewhat manufactured excuse they provoked a row and in true Porsche fashion, the *Herr Doktor Doktor* tore off his hat, stamped it into the snow, and stormed off – this time to work for Steyr. His 100 hp straight-eight Steyr Austria was one of the stars of the 1929 Paris Auto Show, but when Steyr was taken over by Austro-Daimler's bankers (the same ones he had yelled curses at some six or seven years earlier), he was out in the cold again.

This time, he set up on his own: the *Porsche Konstruktionburo für Motoren-Farhrzeug, Luftfahrzeug- und Wasserfahrzeugbau.* His son-in-law Anton Piëch and his old friend Adolf Rosenberger each had 15 per cent of the company, and he had the remaining 70 per cent.

There was no shortage of commissions. The first came from Wanderer (which later merged with Horch, Audi and DKW to form the Auto-Union), and they gave it the project number of seven, so as to conceal the fact that it was their first job. Then came a Zündapp project for a "People's Car," because the then-successful motorcycle company had read the writing on the wall and seen that cheap cars would replace motorcycles in Europe, just as they had in the United States. The Type 12 was only killed because it would have cost too much to put into production. The same happened with a project for NSU. Both cars, though, were clear precursors of the Volkswagen.

Another enthusiast for a people's car was the new Chancellor, one Herr Hitler, and although their initial discussions in 1933 came to nothing, Porsche and Hitler both worked on the idea of a *kleinauto* (small car) for the masses in 1934. They were a strange pair: Porsche almost politically blind, but delighted to have support from so important a man, and the politically astute Hitler at least equally delighted to have such a great man agreeing with him. For all Hitler's faults – and they certainly outweighed his modest array of virtues – it is hard to fault his vision of a Volkswagen.

Because of the Volkswagen project, Hitler was also more than willing to pump money into Porsche's other brainchild, the Auto-Union racers, and so the two projects proceeded side by side.

The Auto-Union racers were built to the simple formula of the period: a dry weight of 1650 lb. (750 kg). Pretty much everything else was open, and while the 1934 models delivered 295 bhp from a supercharged 4.5-liter V-16, power eventually rose to some 600 bhp – a power-to-weight ratio of maybe 750-800 bhp/tonne – which made them the fastest Formula 1 cars of all time. Speeds in excess of 280 mph (say 450 kph) were feasible. The engine was mid-mounted, inside the wheelbase but behind the driver, which reduced the polar moments of inertia and made the handling theoretically safe, but with such a blinding excess of power the chassis could be provoked beyond the ability of anyone but a superman. Caracciola, Stuck and Rosemeyer were arguably supermen, but even Rosemeyer was killed on the *autobahn* when attempting a high-speed run in one of these terrifying machines.

The Volkswagen, or KdF-Wagen (*Kraft durch Freude,* "Strength through Joy") was much less dramatic, though its handling at the limit could be almost equally exciting. The 1131 cc flat-four engine, overhanging the rear axle, drove through a "crash" (non-synchromesh) gearbox and was deliberately understressed to allow it to cruise at 56 mph (90 kph) on the autobahns which had been increasingly widespread in Germany since before Hitler's rise to power. It was economical, basic, and destined to remain in production for decades.

During World War II, Porsche continued to design such *matèriel* as the Elefant tank, as well as wind-powered generators (National Socialism could be quite "Green") and was given honorary SS rank – though, perhaps characteristically, he always managed to avoid being fitted for an SS uniform, and never signed an application for an SS commission. After the war, he was rapidly freed by the Allies, though the French later arrested him .They imprisoned him in an unheated dungeon, despite his advanced years, in an apparent attempt to implicate him as a Nazi and to disguise the truth of their own collaboration, despite his clear anti-Nazi intercession on behalf of Peugeot workers during the war. When he was finally released in mid-1947, it was on payment of bail of FF 500,000, which was never returned despite his acquittal on all charges. The money was raised from the fees earned by the Porsche Design Studio, under his son Ferry, who had just designed a new racer for the Italian firm of Cisitalia.

The 356

The Cisitalia did not go on to become a great name, but another Porsche project did. It started out as a go-faster Volkswagen. Although the Volkswagen did not have a conventional chassis, it had a floor pan which served very much the same purpose, and on which a lighter, sportier

body could be built. The Volkswagen motor, deliberately understressed for durability and cheap maintenance, could easily be persuaded to disburse more power. In retrospect, the 356 seems inevitable, but the path was not a straight one.

Even before the war there had been the Type 64 Volkswagen-based special with its aluminium body, and the 60K10, the latter with a 1500 cc version of the flat-four and 50 bhp. But the original 356/1 did *not* use the Volkswagen floor pan. Instead, it had a tubular space frame, and the engine was effectively rotated about the rear axle to create a mid-engined car. The engine was left at 1131 cc, but given bigger valves, twin carburetors, and a compression ratio of 7:1 instead of 5.8:1, which raised the power to 40 bhp. The whole was clad in a hand-beaten, light-alloy, open body.

It had its problems. The Volkswagen-type suspension was inevitably reversed, and this led to excessive chassis loading and more than usually interesting behavior on corners. Also, space-frames might do for someone like Ferrari, but a floor-pan-type chassis was a lot easier for series production. The result was that 356/2 was a conventionally rear-engined car, and recognizably the ancestor of all other 356 Porsches. It was now a fixed-head coupé (though still with a hand-beaten, light-alloy body), with a remarkably small glass area. On the strength of the 356/2 prototype alone, a Swiss dealer ordered 50 Porsches.

The tiny Porsche operation at Gmünd was simply unable to make cars quickly enough. They built four in 1948 and 25 in 1949. Late in 1949, though, Porsche ordered 500 bodies from Reutter in Stuttgart, with the intention of starting serious production, and these accounted for the bulk of 1950 cars – by the end of the year, 289 had been sold. In October, at the 1950 Paris Auto Show, the banner on the Porsche stand said "1,900 PORSCHE 1950." Just after the show, the *Herr Professor Doktor Doktor* himself suffered a stroke, from which he never fully recovered, and he died on January 30, 1951.

The 356, his brainchild, would, however, continue without him, and as it matured it moved further and further from its Volkswagen roots. In 1951 the brakes became twin-leading-shoe (and hydraulic rather than mechanical, as did the parent Volkswagen), and the engine was first bored to 80 mm for a swept volume of 1286 cc, and then stroked by 10 mm to give 1582 cc. The latter change was accomplished by going over to a built-up crankshaft, because the big end rod bolts would otherwise have contacted the interior of the crankcase. In the following year, bigger, wider drums greatly improved braking, and synchromesh distressed the traditionalists but made the car easier to drive. In another couple of years, the engine options ran from 1086 cc and 40 bhp to 1488 cc and 70 bhp, via most possible combinations of bore and stroke and power output. The American market was offered only the two most powerful models, the 55 bhp 1500 and the 70 bhp 1500S.

With a weight that was still close to 1870 lb (850 kg), and a very aerodynamic body for the period, this made for quite a sporty car. However, a wonderful illustration of how expectations have risen is afforded by comparing the Porsche with just about any mid-range "econobox" of 40 years later, which weighed about the same and had typically 60-70 bhp,

The 356 was beautifully detailed and extremely reliable, and to this day Porsches are probably the only sports cars which are synonymous with reliability. The only problem was that the extreme rear weight bias made the cars somewhat tail-happy, requiring either considerable restraint or enormous skill when negotiating fast bends.

The bodies evolved steadily. The original two-piece windscreen became one-piece, at first "folded" in the middle but then smoothly curved. The wheels shrank from 16 inch to 15 inch, and there were other detail changes. And in addition to the more or less standard fixed-head coupé, both conventional dropheads and the immortal "Speedster" were offered, and, of course, the motors got more powerful.

The 356A of 1955 (the 1956 model year to Americans) was available with two 1300 engines (44 bhp for the plain-bearing, 60 bhp for the roller-bearing), and three flavors of 1600. These were the 60 bhp plain-bearing model (they had redesigned the crankcase) and the 75 bhp 1600S, initially roller-bearing but after September a plain-bearing engine. One roller-bearing motor remained in production: the dry-sump, twin-plugged, four-overhead-cam Carrera motor with an even 100 bhp. This fearsome motor was 100 lb. heavier than the other motors, making the car even more tail-happy than before, with a 41/59 front/rear balance. They called it "Carrera," after the Carrera Panamericana road race from one end of Mexico to the other.

Carrera Speedsters were stripped to the minimum, with even the heater removed to save weight, and had lighter, thinner fenders and plastic windows. With a weight of little more than 1650 lb. (750 kg), the '57 Carrera Speedster had over 130 bhp/tonne, and when they upped the power to 110 bhp for 1958, that figure climbed to well over 140 bhp/tonne. Or you could order the same motor in a respectable fixed-head coupé, with some weight penalty but considerably more comfort and practicality.

While the Speedster was losing weight, the other cars were, however, getting heavier, and the Porsche was losing its sports-racing capability. The answer was an Abarth/Zagato-bodied Abarth Carrera GTL with lavish use of light alloy, and eventually 135 bhp. This was an endurance racer that could be driven on the road.

The 356B was first shown at Frankfurt in September 1961, with much larger windows (which made the old cars look old-fashioned overnight) and anything from 60 bhp with the base 1600 to 130 bhp in the Carrera 2, which was bored to 92 mm for 1966 cc. The Carrera 2 weighed a portly 2288 lb. (1040 kg) but could still comfortably exceed 124 mph (200 kph). Disk brakes stopped the Carrera, while the "cooking" Porsches now had Al-Fin finned drums. Then, less than two years later, the 356C came out with four-wheel disk brakes, and the regular 1600 cc engines were uprated to 75 bhp (1600C) and 95 bhp (1600SC). The construction of the engine had also been updated, with cast-iron liners molded into a light-alloy finned barrel.

But, despite all the improvements, the 356 was becoming outdated. There were still too many links with its Volkswagen ancestry, not least the increasingly dated-looking body. It may be a classic now, but then it was just old-fashioned. Also, Porsche wanted more power, and the pushrod four had been taken about as far as it could go, while the four-overhead-cam engine was just too wild to be made the standard motor. The new engine and the new body came out together, as the 911.

The 911

"Butzi" Porsche, Ferdinand Porsche III, designed the 911. It actually started life as a 901, but Peugeot had registered all numbers with a middle zero as trademarks, so it became a 911.

The engine – which is the important thing in any Porsche – was a flat six of only 1991 cc. As important as the extra cylinders, though, were the overhead cams: one per bank. These, and a forged one-piece crank in eight main bearings, allowed for a stronger, faster-revving engine – the initial power output was 130 bhp, the same as the old Carrera but achieved much more simply and reliably. Broader tires (185/70 VR 15) put the power on the road.

The body was still very much in the Porsche tradition, but somehow much more modern – more squared-off, more glass, more integrated. Although it was heavier than the 356, at 2387 lb. (1086 kg), the extra power still left a comfortable 120 bhp/tonne.

The handling was also very Porsche, and the front end was light (the official factory solution was to bolt cast-iron weights inside the ends of the front bumper), and the car was as tail-happy as ever. However, in all fairness, only fast drivers would ever take the Porsche outside its comfortable performance envelope, and it was an admirably taut car. It went into production in 1964, initially with an all-new five-speed gearbox but then with a four-speed and the five-speed as an option. The car sold like hot cakes, and apart from the light front end and early carburetion troubles (which were slowly overcome), it received little but praise from press and drivers alike.

There was no true convertible, but 1965 saw the "Targa." In the earliest Targas, not only could the top be removed, but the rear window could be zipped out as well, leaving only a big roll bar, but leaks and general unsatisfactoriness led to the rear windows being fixed in later models. April 1965 also saw the 912, which was a 911 body with a Super 90 four-cylinder engine. Although the 90 bhp four was much less smooth than the six, its lighter weight made for a 44/56 front/rear balance instead of 41/59, so there was a chance to make up on the corners what you lost on the straights. This incredibly underrated car is easily the cheapest "classic" Porsche: the first series ran from 1965 to 1969, and the second series of 1975-1977 had a reliable, cheap-to-work-on 1971 cc fuel-injected flat-four from the VW 411 Variant. The only drawback to the second series was that it was an incredible 600 lb. (270 kg) heavier than the first series. In 1965, the original 912 outsold the considerably more expensive 911 by about four to three (6440 to 4865), but basically the problem was making enough Porsches to meet the new demand.

After a pause for breath, though, Porsche started extracting more power from the motor. In July 1966 the 911S offered 160 bhp, courtesy of hotter cams, bigger valves and generally improved breathing, and Weber 40 IDS carburetors. This was four times as much power as the original 356!

As alternatives to the 911S, you could buy the standard 130 bhp 911, the 911T and the 911R. The 911T was actually downrated from the original, with 110 bhp and all kinds of "de-specced" components such as cast-iron cylinders (not light alloy), steel wheels (the 911S had the now trademark,

five-spoke Fuchs alloy wheels, which were five pounds *per wheel* lighter), cast iron instead of steel rocker arms, and so forth. The 911R, on the other hand, was much more powerful and interesting than even the 911S. The body was lightened in every possible way, even down to thinner sheet metal for the body, so it was about 10 per cent lighter than standard (under 2000 lb./900 kg), and the motor was at racing specification with 10.3:1 compression, 46 mm Webers, and 210 bhp: a power-to-weight ratio of better than 230 bhp/tonne. Only 20 cars were made to this specification.

You could also order your Porsche with the "Sportomatic" electro-pneumatic transmission, in which a microswitch built into the gear-lever operated the clutch. It was excessively complicated, and when it failed it was a nightmare to repair.

The subsequent history of the 911 could fill a book of its own. In August 1968, longer rear trailing arms meant a smoother ride, and along with a front-mounted battery contributed to better handling. The front/rear ratio was a slightly less poor 43/57 per cent. Wider wheels were another boon. The basic 911, now the 911E, had 130 bhp while the 911S had 170 bhp, thanks to Bosch mechanical fuel injection.

In September 1969, the C-series engine was bored to give 2195 cc, which gave even the lowly 911T a respectable 125 bhp, and raised the 911E and 911S to 155 bhp and 180 bhp. And then in 1971 the stroke was lengthened from 66 mm to 70.4 mm and the engine expanded to 2341 cc. Even though compression ratios were lowered to allow the new motors to run on "regular" gasoline (93 octane Research, 88 octane R+M/2), power still went on rising, with 140 bhp for the 911T, 165 bhp for the 911E and 190 bhp on the 911S.

Despite the rise in power, the emphasis continued to move away from the stark, sports-racing orientation of the original Porsches and inclined more and more towards creature comforts. The day of the dual-purpose sports-racer was passing anyway, as racers became more and more specialized; the *boulevardier* influence was emphasized by the new layout for the five-speed gearbox. Whereas before the H-gate had been second to fifth, with first out on the dogleg, the new gearbox had first to fourth in the H, with fifth on the dogleg. This was a clear concession to American sensibilities, where snappy, first-second changes were essential for dragster-style starts, while fifth was regarded as an overdrive gear for relaxed cruising. For serious fast driving, of course, one rarely needs first once the car is in motion, and it is useful to be able to switch between fourth and fifth when driving at sustained high speeds, and the United States is a very important market for Porsche.

Even so, there were those at Porsche who thought that you ought to be able to race your car, so in late 1972 the Carrera name was revived for the 911RS (Rennsport) with 210 bhp. The original intention was to build 500 such cars, but because of demand about 1000 were built to full *Rennsport* specification, with drastically reduced weight of just under 2000 lb. (over 900 kg), and 600 more were made as "go-faster" 911S models. The engine was bored yet again, to 90 mm, to get the extra power, but the pistons now had to run in Nickasil bores, because the old Biral cylinders were on the edge at about 87-88 mm. A "ducktail" spoiler, looking uncommonly like an afterthought, helped to keep these cars on the road at the very high speeds of which they were capable. If the 911RS was still not enough for you, the 911RSR was a go-faster 911RS. Bored to 2806 cc, it had over 300 bhp, and won the Targa Florio in 1975.

The 2687 cc Nickasil-bore motor was standardized for the 1974 model year, but this was the year of the so-called "gas crisis" and Porsche nodded in the direction of the fashionable hysteria of the period by reducing power to 150 bhp for the "cooking" 911, and 175 bhp for the 911S and the Carrera. As consolations, they also offered the 911RS (230 bhp) and the 911RSR (330 bhp with the slide-valve carbs, 315 bhp with butterfly valves). A total of 109 RS and RSR models were made, 49 as out-and-out racers, and 60 as road cars – though not always in the form of fully sound-insulated and fully-trimmed road cars. And in 1975 the Carrera got its power back, at 210 bhp.

This was, however, small beer next to the 260 bhp Turbo, the 2993 cc engine in its ultimate form for the 1975 model year. Acceleration was blinding, top speed was hair-raising at over 150 mph (close to 250 kph), and it hardly seemed that more was possible.

But of course it was. Not much happened to the engines until 1978, though the body was at last rustproofed in 1976, rust having been a besetting sin of all previous Porsches. But the '78 Turbo delivered 300 bhp from an engine that had been bored to 97 mm and stroked to 74.4 mm for a swept volume of 3299 cc. Top speed was now over 170 mph (about 275 kph), and the 0-60 time was 5.3 seconds. The 911SC was upgraded to 180 bhp, but somehow, the Turbo took everyone's attention.

By the late 1970s, an interesting new phenomenon started to appear. No longer was America the most important market: in 1979, and more Porsches were sold in Germany alone than in the United States. As a result, Americans became the "poor relations," because it was not worth tailoring cars to a market where government-mandated "safety" standards and smog laws were guaranteed to emasculate *really* fast cars. The 911 was continued, but not as the cutting-edge road car. That honor went to the 959, which may have looked fairly like a 911, but which owed at least as much to the 935 racer. The 959 had a Kevlar composite body, electronically-controlled four-wheel-drive with continuously variable front/rear traction splitting, and a twin-turbo engine delivering a minimum of 400 bhp and driving through a six-speed gear box. In road trim it cracked the 186 mph (300 kph) barrier with ease. Porsche never produced an American version – it was simply too much trouble – though they did offer a cosmetic/aerodynamic package which at least made a 911 look like a 959.

The 959 was, however, a little on the wild side as a production car, and so for 1989 Porsche at last revised the 911 chassis and placed a new car on it, the 911 Carrera 4. This was a four-wheel-drive Carrera, with electronically-controlled locking differentials and anti-lock braking as standard. A rear spoiler automatically rose at about 40 mph (65 kph), and then automatically folded away again at about six mph (10 kph).

The old floor pan continued as the underpinning for the new Speedster (of which only 800 were made, principally for the California market) and the Club Sport, a seriously lightened 911 Carrera coupé with the "junk" (air conditioning, electric door locks, electric windows, etc.) deleted for a significant 155 lb. (70 kg) weight saving.

The new pan was next used for the Carrera 2, a two-wheel-drive derivative of the Carrera 4, and then for the 911 Turbo Coupé, a 315 bhp car that could reach 62 mph (100 kph) in five seconds and nudge 170 mph (270 kph) flat out. The motor was twin-plugged, to allow it to run on *very* ordinary fuel, and the whole plot was even made available to the long-suffering Americans.

The old "R" designation was also revived in the early 1990s for a lightened, extra-powerful 911 with 380 bhp to propel a mere 2816 lb. (1280 kg): not quite 300 bhp/tonne, and 62 mph (100 kph) from a standing start in 4.7 seconds.

Although the seemingly immortal 911 series still shows its 356 and even Volkswagen ancestry, it is nevertheless true that it is, and always has been, in many ways state of the art, and in other ways downright eccentric. For example, the Carrera 2 introduced a strange new gearbox, the "Tiptronic" which looked something like a conventional H-gate. On the left, though, the lever functions as a conventional four-speed automatic, and on the right it functions rather like a motorcycle gearbox – a brisk pull backwards changes down one gear, while a smart push forwards changes up one gear. The change is obviously far quicker than on a true automatic, but is it the wave of the future, or is it another Sportomatic?

The 914

To justify its complexity, lack of luggage space, and other drawbacks, a mid-engined car must be very, very quick or extremely beautiful, or preferably both. The 914 was neither.

It was an unhappy hybrid from the start. It was conceived as a replacement for the VW Karmann Ghia, which may have its admirers but which is not widely praised for its handsomeness. The idea was that Porsche would design it, Volkswagen would build it, and Porsche would buy back some of the body shells to turn into "Volksporsches." The only catch was that when Kurt Lotz took over at Volkswagen on the death of Heinz Nordhof, he demanded such a high price for the body shells that Porsche decided, after only 3360 Porsche-engined 914/6 cars, to cut their losses and cease production.

The specifications of the 914/6 looked good. With the 110 bhp two-liter flat six of the 911T, it was about 198 lb. (90 kg) lighter than even the original 911, and the 46/54 front/rear weight distribution was a marked improvement on any 911. Or to look at it another way, it was identical in weight to the original 912 at 2189 lb. (995 kg), but had the 110 bhp six instead of the 90 bhp four. It was far from a slug, and it cost about half as much as any 911.

It was, however, dragged down by a number of factors. The most obvious was the 914/4, with its 80 bhp Volkswagen pushrod engine. While there was a 121 lb. (55 kg) weight saving, and an even better front/rear balance, the power-to-weight ratio of 85 bhp/tonne represented a considerable step backwards to 1950s levels. Equally important was the extreme ugliness of the car, and these two problems reared their heads even before anyone considered test driving a 914.

Assuming they did get into the driving seat, the test driver soon learned that these were not the only faults. The seats

were non-adjustable, the cockpit was cramped, noisy and inclined to overheat, luggage space was negligible, gear selection was imprecise, and the whole car simply fell short in every department when compared with a "real" Porsche, except in rapid cornering. In addition, the 914/4 had an infuriating habit of refusing to restart when it was switched off after fast driving, and had to be left to cool down. The two main problems were fuel vapor lock and electrical vagaries. The later 914/4, after the passing of the 914/6, was a rather better car with a 95 bhp flat-four, a much better gear-shift linkage, and an adjustable driver's seat.

The net result was that although the 914/4 was far from a failure – over 127,000 were built – it was far from a success either. The saga of the 914 is, therefore, an interesting one of what might have been, as there were some very interesting 914 derivatives, which could possibly have overcome the car's ugliness by redeeming it with sheer quickness.

A 160 bhp racing derivative of the 914/6, the 914/6GT, won its class at Le Mans in 1970 as well as taking first, second and third places (the old Porsche trick) in the Marathon de la Route in the same year. This led to the idea of a redesigned 914, the 916. Big, rectangular flares over the wide wheels gave the car a much more purposeful look, as did a self-colored integrated front bumper and front spoiler. The car was "cleaned up" with less chrome, and was powered by the 155 bhp version of the 2.4-liter fuel-injected motor, as fitted to the 911E. It was very slightly heavier than the 914/6 at 2200 lb (exactly 1000 kg), but 155 bhp/tonne and excellent handling could have made the car a success. In fact, about 20 were built and a brochure was printed up for the 1971 Paris Motor Show, but the car was cancelled, and the logical inference is that it was still too close to the 914/4, with which Porsche did not want to be too closely associated. Various members of the Porsche family and a few special customers received the 916 cars that were made.

There was also a 914/8, or, to be precise, there were two of them. They were 914's fitted with the three-liter flat-eight racing engine, and they were presented to Ferry Porsche and Ferdinand Piëch. While these were by no means feasible as production vehicles, they showed that there were those at Porsche who took the whole mid-engine concept very seriously, and that it would have been possible to develop the 914 as a very serious fast motor car – a 914/6 Carrera would by no means have been out of the way.

In the end, though, it came down to somewhat strained relations between Volkswagen and Porsche, and to the almost irremediable ugliness of the body. The 914 is really just a footnote to the history of both Porsche and Volkswagen, and there must have been those at Porsche who wished they had never put their company's name on the thing.

Straight Fours and V-Eights

The original 356 had evolved from the basic Volkswagen, and the 911 had evolved from the 356. But there is a not unreasonable fear at Porsche that, despite all evidence to the contrary, the 911 cannot go on forever.

The 914 represented, to some extent, a return to Porsche's roots as a light, fast car, and that, as much as its ugliness, may have been a part of its undoing. The steady increase in the weight of the 911 is explained in part by the need to strengthen parts to handle ever more power, but also from the increasing creature comforts that are provided for the driver. The 924, therefore, was conceived as a rather heavier car from the outset.

The company's close relationship with Volkswagen has always given them considerable access to Volkswagen's parts bin, and of course they have worked together with Volkswagen on a number of projects. The 924 began life as Volkswagen EA425, a flagship for the new generation of front-wheel-drive Volkswagens which included the Passat and Polo. In fact, there had already been a much more interesting EA266, with a water-cooled four lying on its side under the rear seat, but Rudolf Leiding at Volkswagen was an ardent believer in front wheel drive, so EA266 never got anywhere.

Then Tony Schmücker replaced Rudolf Leiding and EA425 was also knocked on the head: it was too expensive, too powerful, too flagrant to introduce in the wake of the so-called "gas crisis." But he had no objection to Porsche continuing with the project, which was 924 in their notation. It also suited his book to let them have the old NSU plant at Neckarsulm, which he had been planning to close as another cost-saving exercise. At the end of the day, everyone came out well from the complex string of deals, and Porsche had a rather handsome body-shell with only one drawback – they did not want a front-wheel-drive car.

In the long run, they had in mind a really powerful engine, and trying to feed Porsche-style power through the front wheels alone was just not on. They therefore needed a front-engine, rear-drive car, which ran them into the problems of a too-heavy front end, the exact opposite of the problem with the 911. They solved their difficulties by the elegant expedient of using a rear transaxle, which gave a 48/52 per cent front/rear balance – significantly better than even the 914.

The motor, though, was less exciting. It was essentially an Audi design (Volkswagen and Audi now formed VAG, the Volkswagen-Audi Group), and as a sohc straight-four of 1984 cc it was nothing remarkable. The power in European trim was an acceptable 125 bhp, but with American emission controls on it, 100 bhp was all that was under the driver's right foot. The weight of the car was kept to a very respectable 2376 lb. (1080 kg), so the power-to-weight ratio of the European cars was close to 116 bhp/tonne, but the American model was, for Porsche, a miserable 93 bhp/tonne. The transaxle was also Audi, and other parts came from Volkswagens, Audis and even the venerable Beetle, with its trailing arms at the back, the MacPherson strut at the front, and the rear drums.

The Porsche 924 entered production in November 1975, and immediately provoked howls of agony and rage from the purists in a way that even the 914 had not done. The engine was in the wrong place (the middle was acceptable, the front wasn't) and it was cooled by the wrong fluid (water instead of oil – anyone who thinks flat-six Porsches are air-cooled has never seen the size of the oil coolers). The American press panned it because the ride was too harsh, and transmitted too much road noise. And everyone agreed that the engine sounded rather busy if you pressed on too enthusiastically. Never mind the 125 mph (effectively 200 kph) top speed, the 0-60 time of 8.2 seconds, or the very modest fuel consumption (11 liters/100 km, 25 mpg imperial, 20 mpg American). It just wasn't Porsche enough.

For 1977 the four-speed gearbox was replaced with a five-speed in the *Getrag* layout (first in the dogleg). This eased complaints about high-speed engine noise, and the 1979 modification which placed fifth in the dogleg kept the Americans happy. A much more important 1979 change, though, was the availability of a turbo model. The weight went up somewhat, by 225 lb. (102 kg), but the power went up dramatically to 170 bhp for the European market and 150 bhp for the emission-strangled Americans. This meant power-to-weight ratios of 144 bhp/tonne and 127 bhp/tonne respectively.

Also in 1977, the 928 was announced, and this was a much more interesting use for the same body shell. In place of the rather pedestrian four, there was a 4.5-liter all-alloy V-8 with linerless bores. Although the V-8 was hardly a revolutionary format, and although it disappointed those who wanted a flat-eight or a V-12, it had the advantage of fitting neatly into the same engine bay as the straight four.

The single overhead cam on each bank of cylinders was driven by a toothed belt, rather than by the chains of the flat six; belts are quieter, cheaper, and require less maintenance than chains, though they have to be changed periodically for total reliability. The 90 mm bore and 78.9 mm stroke gave an actual swept volume of 4474 cc, from which the first version of the engine extracted 240 bhp, a mere 53.6 bhp/liter, so one could tell that there was room for plenty of development work. The American version was only slightly less powerful, at 230 bhp (51.4 bhp/liter). As a matter of interest, the contemporary Corvette offered 225 bhp from 5735 cc, or 39.2 bhp/liter, though that figure might have risen to the low forties after allowing for the difference between SAE net and DIN horsepower figures. The Corvette also weighed 3655 lb. (1661 kg) against the Porsche's 3200 lb. (1450 kg).

Although the purists still rent their clothes and tore their hair, everyone else was much more impressed with the 928. At 165 bhp/tonne, it offered a significant amount of power, and the front-rear balance was excellent. Fifth-gear was straight through (the 924 transmission was all-indirect), with a high final drive and, to keep the weight down, the doors, hood and front fenders were of light alloy; otherwise, the new Porsche could have weighed as much as the Corvette. There were, however, power windows, air conditioning, and pneumatic central locking, as well as other luxury-car features which were lacking on most cars with this kind of performance.

In 1979 the 928 was bored out to 92 mm and given improved breathing, both in and out, as well has having its compression ratio raised from 9:1 to 10:1. This gave a nice, round 300 bhp and a top speed of about 155 mph (250 kph) for the new 928S. The drag coefficient, or C_d, was lowered to 0.38, which was tolerable but not remarkable, and the following year the car actually lost 220 lb. (100 kg) by more extensive use of light alloys and clever production engineering. In the same year – 1980 – the regular 928S gained a whole one bhp to 231 bhp, but Americans could not buy the 928S – there was just no point in going through the homologation hoops when Porsche could sell all the cars they could make

in less protected markets.

Not until 1985 did the long-suffering Americans get extra power, and this only happened when the engine sprouted two more cams and was bored out to exactly 100 mm, for a swept volume of 4957 cc. Even the Americans were permitted 300 bhp, while Europeans got more; steady development got it up to about 350 bhp, around 70 bhp/liter and over 230 bhp/tonne. In 1987 some serious attention to the aerodynamics got the C_d down to 0.35 and produced a top speed of 165 mph (268 kph) for the manual version or 162 mph (250 kph) for the automatic.

Meanwhile, the hoi polloi *had* not been forgotten. For those who could not afford (or could persuade themselves they did not need) the V-8, there was a brand-new four. It was still a sohc design, but the capacity went up to 2479 cc. The bore and stroke were identical to the V-8 at 100 mm x 78.9 mm, but it was still a long way from half a V-8. In particular, the inherent lumpiness of a big, powerful four was tamed by using Mitsubishi-patented contra-rotating balance shafts. Base power was 160 bhp for the European market, 150 bhp for the Americans.

Further to reduce the risk of vibration, both the engine and the transmission were rubber mounted. The engine mounts were particularly weird, containing as they did two small chambers filled with anti-freeze and connecting via a narrow passage: the incompressible anti-freeze meant that the whole mount acted as a damper-cum-shock-absorber.

To emphasize the difference between the old 924 and the new car, it was called a 944. It is impossible not to suspect that Porsche's project numbering system had to be bent slightly to create a four-cylinder 924, an eight-cylinder 928, and a four-cylinder 944.

Regardless of any such chicanery, the 944 was immediately accepted by all but the most stalwart 911 diehards. Of course, it benefited immensely by being compared with the somewhat anemic 924, rather than with the seemingly immortal 911 or with the frankly irrelevant 914. It offered just about everything the 928 did, with the exception of power, and because of the reduced weight of the four, it weighed only 2530 lb. (1150 kg) and therefore offered 139 bhp/tonne.

What happened next was absolutely predictable to any student of Porsches. First, in 1985 they turbocharged the original sohc engine to give 220 bhp and a top speed of significantly over 150 mph (240 kph) and 0-60 mph times in the low sixes.

Then, in 1986 the 944S appeared. This was a twin-cam, 16-valve design without a turbocharger, but now delivering 188 bhp and a top speed only about 10 mph (16 kph) slower than the Turbo. And then, of course, they turbocharged that, to create the 944 Turbo S, with a top speed of over 160 mph (around 260 kph) and a 0-60 time of about five-and-a-half seconds.

At this point, the engine was delivering very close to 100 bhp/liter, which is the maximum that most people normally expect from any engine, so it was time to make it larger. The sohc models were bored to 103.8 mm for 2682 cc, and the dohc models were bored and stroked to give 2990 cc. The 1989 S2 delivered 208 bhp without a turbocharger.

In 1991 the 944 S2 was replaced by the 968, which Porsche trumpeted as a new car but which should in all fairness be regarded as a significantly improved 944. The body borrowed some front-end styling from the 911, and a number of other features from the rest of the 944/968 range, and the C_d came down to 0.34 (which was pretty unimpressive by this time), but the 3014 lb. (1370 kg) bulk of the "new" car was propelled by a 240 bhp derivative of the long-suffering big four. The conventionally-aspirated engine featured variable valve timing, and fed through a *six*-speed box which allowed a top speed of 156 mph (rather over 250 kph). Some thought the styling looked dated, while others called it classic, and there were those who reckoned it looked merely indecisive. The dropped nose, with its clear homage to the 911, made the passenger compartment look rather bulbous, like a late E-type Jaguar with a flattened engine compartment.

Almost simultaneously, the 928 GTS appeared, a new top-of-the-line V8 bored out to no less than 5.4 liters and delivering 350 bhp for a power-to-weight ratio of about 216 bhp/tonne. Running on huge, 17-inch wheels, the biggest of the 928 series could hit 170 mph (just about 275 kph) and combined luxury with such aids to serious motoring as an electronically-controlled limited slip differential.

No sooner had the 928 GTS been launched than the motoring press began to speculate that it might be the swan song of the old 924/928/944/968 line. After all, essentially the same body had been in production for almost 17 years by that time, and Porsche was no longer quite so pre-eminent in the field of well-built, luxurious, seriously fast cars. Jaguars had been improved dramatically, BMWs were getting more luxurious, Mercedes were returning to serious performance sporting cars, and the Japanese were making their presence felt very strongly indeed. What all of those manufacturers lacked, though, was the kind of racing and "supercar" reputation that Porsche had built and maintained solidly for more than half a century, ever since their inception in the late 1940s.

Sports Racers and Exotica

On July 11, 1948, Porsche prototype 356/1 took a class win at a round-the-houses race at Innsbruck. Note that well. The very first Porsche ever built was raced, and won its class.

By 1950, when there were still fewer than 50 Porsches on the road, Prince Joachim zu Furstenberg and Count Constantin Berckheim won the 1100 cc class and Countess Cecilia Koskull took the Ladies' Award at the Midnight Sun Rally. At the Interlaken International Rally, Count von der Muhle-Eckhart and Rudolph Sauerwein won their class and came second overall. And in 1951, the first "works" entry was Le Mans, where Porsche won their class award and came 20th overall. The "class" in question in each case was the 750-1100 cc class, for which the bore of the 1131 cc engine had to be reduced to 73.5 mm, giving 1086 cc. Such stories could be repeated indefinitely, but a catalog of Porsche wins would soon become repetitive and would in any case be of limited interest. Only the highlights will be reported here.

Highlights such as the class and world records established in 1951, when a 62 bhp alcohol-burning 1100 took the class records for 500 miles, 1000 km, and six hours – all at over 100 mph (160 kph). An open 1500 took the same records at 114.3 to 116.6 mph (184.35 to 188.06kph), while the ex-Le Mans 1500 won the 1500 cc record for 72 hours. Despite losing first, second and fourth gears on the third day, they still averaged 94.66 mph (152.67 kph) for the whole 72 hours, covering 6,8515.5 miles (10,904.8 km) and establishing a new *world* record . . .

Highlights like 1100 cc class wins in the 1952 Mille Miglia and at Le Mans in the same year, or coming first, third and fourth overall at the Liege-Rome-Liege rally in the same year, or taking eight out of ten class placings at the *Ballon d'Alsace* hill-climb ....

The trouble was that these were the very last days of the true sports-racer, when wealthy young men or women would tape the headlights of their road cars and race them on the track. The cars that would win in future were often completely unsuitable for the road, with no luggage space, minimal weather protection, passenger seats that were merely nominal, and bodywork of thin, hand-beaten light alloy which simply would not stand up to parking lot abuse. The rules were repeatedly rewritten to make the racers more like sports cars, but the manufacturers (Porsche more than many) would then find the loopholes with the astuteness of canon or Chancery lawyers.

The first cataloged Porsche racer (unless you count the 356SL Le Mans replica) was the 550. At the car's first outing at Nurburgring on May 31, 1953, they won. At Le Mans, they came first and second in their class and 15th and 16th overall. At the end of the season both factory prototypes were sold to Jaroslav Juhan, who achieved a class win with one of them in the Carrera Panamericana in Mexico. Then, with the four-overhead-cam 547 engine replacing the old roller-bearing 1500, a 550 won its class and came sixth overall in the '54 Mille Miglia, to say nothing of first and second in class and third and fourth overall in the '54 Carrera, the last to be held in its original form (it was revived as a vintage event decades later). The 547 engine was fiendishly complicated, with shaft-and-spur-driven cams with the camshaft drive in the middle of the engine, between the cylinders. It typically took a minimum of eight hours just to set up the timing on one of these twin-plugged monsters. A roadgoing 550 was known as a 1500RS – James Dean was driving one when he died.

Then, in 1956, the space-frame 550A arrived with immensely better handling. Its party-piece was winning the Targa Florio outright, against such competition as a 300S Maserati and a Monza Ferrari. A class win and fifth overall followed at Le Mans, and these incredible cars were still getting class wins in the early 1960s.

Unless, of course, there were other Porsches in the running. The 718 (or RSK) managed a second in the Targa Florio and third overall at Le Mans, where they also got a two-liter class win with a 1600 cc motor and a 1500 cc class win with the 1500. The Targa Florio was another outright win, this time in '59. Transmuted into the R60, the RSK won the 1960 Targa Florio outright, as well as an absolute win at Sebring.

The next real landmark was in 1963, when the 547 engine was inserted into the new 904 sports/racer and took both first and second at the 1964 Targa Florio. At Le Mans in '64, both works 904s dropped out (they had the three-liter flat-eight from the unsuccessful Formula 1 program) but over-the-counter versions entered privately came in seventh, eighth, tenth, eleventh and twelfth. Before they dropped out, though,

the 904/8s were timed at 175 mph (over 282 kph) on the Mulsanne straight. There was also a 904/6, but it did no better than the 904/8s.

The 904/4 was very beautiful, and just about street legal, but you would have had to be a masochist to drive it. The parting of street and track really came in a big way with the 906 in 1966. These cars made hardly any concessions to street legality, with the huge rear engine cover held in place by external fasteners and a vast, louvered "rear window" which had very little of the real world about it. The 906 appeared with a number of engines, up to and including the flat-eight – which still had a capacity of under two liters. At Le Mans in 1966 the 906/8 took fourth, fifth, sixth, seventh and eighth places. The Ford GT40s which took first, second and third, had seven-liter engines, so there was a certain disparity of size at work!

The 910 was the next out-and-out racer, in 1967. Like the 906, it was a 904 derivative and could accept either the flat-six or the flat-eight. The small engines were, however, proving to be a handicap: the sheer, raw power of the bigger cars was something with which they could not compete. The 907 actually appeared after the 910, and did not do particularly well at Le Mans but won the Targa Florio, despite having to stop to recapture a wheel which came off.

The 908 was a response to the new CSI rules for 1968 (the CSI was the forerunner of the FIA, and equally Gallic and chauvinist), and consisted of a three-liter dohc flat-eight wrapped in a car which could hit 190 mph on the Mulsanne straight, but was distinctly short on stability. Although there were successes in '68, including an outright win at the 'Ring with a *kurzheck* (short-tail) version, it was not until 1969 that the 908 started to win in a big way: 1-2-3 at the BOAC 500 at Brands Hatch, 1-2-3-4 at the Targa Florio, and 1-2-3-4-5 at the Nurburgring. At Le Mans only one car could beat the 908 – the Gulf Ford, with more than twice the engine capacity. Still, second place isn't winning.

The 917 was not designed for second place. It was essentially a bigger, stronger 908 with 50 per cent more cylinders and 50 per cent more capacity: a 4.5-liter flat-twelve delivering at least 450 bhp. Because it had to be a cataloged production car with a production run of at least 25, Porsche built 25 of them (in 10 months!) and cataloged them at DM140,000.

It had the faults of the 908 as well as its qualities. The very first 917 to be sold was fatally crashed at Le Mans in 1969, but the top speed defied belief – one 917 was clocked at 236 mph (393 kph) on the Mulsanne straight, about 10 per cent faster than anything else, ever. Although a 917 won easily at the Osterreichring 1000, it was clear that more development was going to be needed.

The Gulf-sponsored John Wyer racing team was given management responsibilities, and 1970 showed the results of both technical and management development. The jewel in the crown was – at last – an outright win at Le Mans, but out of the 24 Championship races for 1970 Porsche won 15 in 917s and a further four in 908s, leaving five winning slots for all other manufacturers combined.

Once they had the knack of Le Mans, they won again in 1971, and turned their attention to the Can-Am series. With 5347 cc and 660 bhp in the old faithful 917, they were in contention, but the 780 bhp of the McLaren Chevrolets showed that brute power was where it was at, and so Porsche turbocharged the beast for 1000 bhp peak, and won easily. The next year, they had 1100 bhp as the baseline, with peak readings of 1500 bhp. They won. The rules were smartly changed, and Porsche gracefully withdrew.

Now comes the funny bit, they decided that the 911 could be made into a fast car. Anyone who thought it was fast before would have difficulty in recognizing it in its new incarnation.

The 300 bhp 911 RSR has already been mentioned; it won the very last Targa Florio, perhaps an entirely fitting end to a race that had been a Porsche stamping ground since long before there were Porsches. For 1974 they found 30 more ponies in the RSR somewhere, and brought it up to 330 bhp. Then, for the same season, they dropped the capacity of the six to 2.14-liters, which, with the addition of a turbocharger, made it the equivalent of a three-liter in the eyes of the FIA. The result was 450 bhp. Only steering and gearbox problems held the Turbo Carrera down to second place at Le Mans. The following year, the best that Porsche could do at Le Mans (with the normally-aspirated three-liter) was fourth.

In 1976, though, they used the 930 (clearly a 911 derivative) in various guises: the turbocharged 485 bhp 934 even had the stock 911 electric windows to help bring it up to the minimum weight requirement, while the 935 had a 911 floor pan with a glass fiber/polyurethane sandwich body, and titanium coil springs. With its turbocharged 2856 cc engine it could compete in the same class as unblown four-liter cars, and it delivered 590 bhp. The ultimate derivative, the 936, had a space frame and a 917-like body. At Le Mans a 936 was first overall, a 935 dominated Group 5 and a 934 took Group 4, "limited-production touring cars."

In 1977 it was more of the same. Porsche won every single round of the World Championship of Makes (like Group 5, essentially modified production cars) and every single round of the Can-Am series – and of course Le Mans, albeit in a 936 that finished on five cylinders because one piston had a hole in it. For 1978 the 935 acquired a tubular frame and lost the majority of its 911 ancestry, and went right on winning.

Almost as an aside, to inject a little interest into the two-liter class (where Ford had previously had a chance), Porsche built a 935/2 for the 1977 season and fitted it with a turbocharged 1.4-liter engine delivering 370 bhp . . .

Thereafter, Le Mans is as good a barometer of Porsche performance as any. A 936/77 replica was the highest placed car in 1980, and came second, but in 1981 the Ickx/Bell 936 won again, fitted with a 2650 cc engine which had originally been developed for Indianapolis but which never raced because of a rule change. It won by four whole laps.

In 1982, the 956 – a monocoque with the Indy engine – came in 1-2-3 (in team order, they did their lap of honor before the race was over) followed by 935s in fourth and fifth place. In '83, they filled nine out of the first ten places. Without any works cars in '84, privateers took eight out of the first ten places. In '85, the same car that had won the previous year won again, and another 956 came second, a works 962, a 956 derivative, came third. For '86 it was 962s in first and second place, with a 956 third – Porsche's sixth consecutive Le Mans win.

The '87 Daytona, though, was the last major race when Porsches were allowed to have everything their own way, with 962s taking 1-2-3-4-5-6; and since then Porsche has concentrated on privateers. With the slump of the late 1980s and early 1990s, there was not in any case the cash available for racing. Porsche sales fell dramatically, and there was constant talk of their selling out to another company. Mercedes Benz were reported to have a standing offer to buy the company for a few *billion* Deutschmarks – Porsche would fit in very well with their revived racing program – and both the Volkswagen-Audi Group and BMW were other logical contenders. Jaguar's racing program put quite a dent in Porsche's success, and the Japanese were looking ever stronger.

Of course, one cannot write Porsche off. The 959, another 911 derivative, with electronically-controlled four-wheel drive, was first and second (and sixth) in the 1986 Paris-Dakar, and they have done well in many other rally/road race events. But they don't have the sheer glory of the out-and-out racers, and Lancia and the Japanese were making inroads there, too.

When all is said and done, though, the extraordinary combination of racing prowess and reliability is what has kept Porsches uniquely desirable. To be sure, there have been slow Porsches, there have been ill-handling Porsches, there have even (occasionally) been somewhat corpulent Porsches. But with that racing ideal always before them, they have never succumbed to the ordinary.

It is impossible to write an up-to-date book about Porsches. Even the old favorites are constantly revised, improved, made faster. And always the rumor mill is suggesting new Porsches – new combinations of existing technology (the application of variable valve timing to the V8 was widely predicted), or even completely new vehicles. Some have a clear basis in reality, like the four-door 989, but either disappear before they go into production or remain out of sight for so long that everyone thinks they have disappeared.

Possibly the oil-cooled boxers will ultimately be finished off by ever more stringent noise regulations, though there is no reason why water-cooled boxers should not replace them – whether they are flat-fours, flat-sixes or even flat-eights. The coolant jackets, of course, muffle noise as well as removing surplus heat. The magazines have published pictures of what they say are 911 look-alikes with water-cooled engines, though they are unable to agree on whether they are fitted with V8s or with flat motors.

And as for the 996 "replacement" for the 911, or the mid-engined 986, well, we shall have to see whether anything truly replaces anything else, or whether it withers on the vine like the 914 or runs concurrently like the 928. One thing is for sure, though: barring very nasty surprises, Porsche will continue to delight drivers for many years to come.

PORSCHE
STUTTGART

Where it all began: a 1948 356/2, its Volkswagen ancestry very clear in the bulbous hubcaps, the tiny glass area (with a split screen), the spindly windshield wipers... Also, unlike its great contemporary the Ferrari (likewise launched in 1947/48), the body is practical rather than stylish.

The interior of the Gmund-built 356/2 seems somewhat claustrophobic today, with its high, small windows. The interior is Spartan, with modest instrumentation set in a

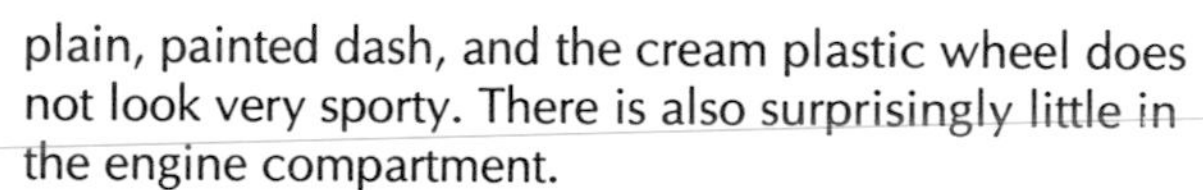

plain, painted dash, and the cream plastic wheel does not look very sporty. There is also surprisingly little in the engine compartment.

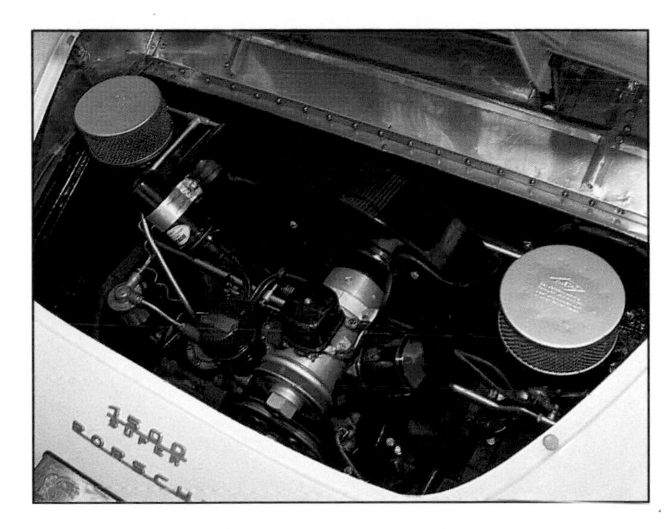

By 1952, when this 1500 Super America was made, the engine compartment was already beginning to look distinctly more crowded and purposeful, and the passenger compartment was very much more luxurious, with a much wider range of instruments and seats shaped to give better support. This car also has several period add-on goodies, including the hood straps, wheel trims and headlight stone guards.

PORSCHE

This 1954 356/1500 shows still more luxury on the inside, with winding windows, properly upholstered bucket seats, and "clocks" that go the right way – on the earliest models, the speedometer ran anti-clockwise. Also, this speedo reads to 120 mph (about 195 kph) – the original ran to only 150 kph. But the 4500 rpm "blood line," with 5000 rpm available for emergencies, still betrays the Volkswagen ancestry.

PORSCHE

M.P.H.
VDO
U/min
×100
VDO

Each year, the Porsches improved. Not only does this 1955 356/1500 look much better balanced than the previous convertible, it also has better, easier-to-read instruments and a one-piece windshield for improved forward visibility.

PORSCHE

PORSCHE

To this day, the original Speedster is one of the most desirable and sought-after of all Porsches: this is a very early one. The lightweight, stripped-out body by Reutter of Stuttgart is beautifully set off here by the faired-in mirrors, the chromed stone guards over the recessed headlights, and the flat hubcaps with the Porsche insignia. The brilliant red paint helps, too! Weighing as little as 1650 lb, a Speedster is a reminder that power-to-weight ratios are about weight as well as power.

A Speedster never really looks right with the top on: the vestigial hood is the merest concession to the slight risk that you might be caught in the rain in Southern California. The 1600S engine was the most powerful engine of 1955 (except for the racing Carrera), and delivered 75 bhp – exactly 100 bhp/tonne. The real clue to the increased power can be seen on the rev counter: the blood line is at 7000 rpm, with brief excursions to 7500 permitted.

PORSCHE
NOV
CALIFORNIA
DDC 580

Barely recognizable as a Porsche, this 1955 550 Spyder is nevertheless a derivative of the 356. The first cataloged Porsche racer, it began its career in 1953 by winning, at the Nurburgring, the very first race in which it was ever entered. What is fascinating is that it is a true dual-purpose sports/racing car, a breed that no longer exists today. You could literally drive it to the track, tape the headlights, and start dicing – with every intention, and expectation, of winning. In normal roadgoing form it was known as a 1500RS; it was in one of these that James Dean died, just outside Cholame, apparently unable to the last to believe that the other driver had not seen him. Note the big rapid-filler cap in front of the windshield – in those days, racers were commonly refueled with a wide-mouthed funnel.

PORSCHE

26

The 356B of 1959 was the second restyle of the original 356. The much larger glass area made the previous generation look old-fashioned overnight, while the engines ranged from a base 60 bhp to a maximum of 130 bhp; this 1600 Super had 90 bhp, and a modest 5000 rpm blood line.

There may not be too much space for luggage under the nose, but who would complain? A proper, wood-rimmed steering wheel instead of a plastic ex-Volkswagen part, and styling which at last looked as if it was meant to be that way, instead of being a Volks that had shrunk in the wash – who would not want to see a 356B outside their door, beckoning?

PORSCHE

KAROSSERIEWERKE DRAUZ K.G. HEILBRONN a/N
Custom Coachwork
BY DRAUZ
KAROSSERIE HEILBRONN
GERMANY

In the interests of aerodynamics, the recessed headlights were covered with an outer glass shell, and increasing integration of details such as indicator and brake lights showed that the 356B had come a long way from a Volkswagen-derived "special."

BMX 720A

The bigger "greenhouse" is much more obvious in this 1963 fixed-head 356B (also overleaf) than in the roadster on the previous pages. The "90" refers to the brake horsepower of the 1600 cc motor. Many people regard the 356B as the definitive 356 – the 356C is sometimes seen as a "stopgap" while waiting for the 911.

BMX 720A

This 1964 Carrera 904 GTS is a very much more modern looking vehicle than the 356, and rather more mainstream than the contemporary 911. On the other hand, it is clear that this is primarily a racer that can (just about) be driven on the road, provided you don't mind deafening noise, a somewhat rudimentary body, and a distinctly bare, functional and echoing interior. But who among us could not put up with that, in return for owning the last car with the four-cam 547 engine?

Carrera
GTS

Carrera
GTS

The 904 was one of those rare designs that just looked right from every angle. As well as being fitted with the flat-four engine, it was also tried with the six and even the Formula 1 eight.

PORSCHE 904

The very earliest Targas had zip-out rear windows as well as removable roof panels, but later models had a considerably more weatherproof fixed rear window. This 1973 2.4 liter 911T shows how little the 911 had changed since its introduction in 1964, though compared with a modern 911 the wheels are very narrow, there is hardly any flare on the wheel-arches, and the whole car looks severe and stark. The "T" engine, at 125 bhp, was the lowest-rated power unit when this car was made, and on the early "T" models steel wheels were standard instead of the now-trademark five-spoked Fuchs alloy wheels.

The 914 was Porsche's "ugly duckling" – this is a 1974 model. Mid-engined two-seaters are notoriously difficult to style, and Porsche made the mistake of assuming that they could get away with a brutally simple, functional look. Front/rear balance is superb, but unfortunate looks and disregard for driver comfort and convenience doomed the 914.

The trouble with any "Targa" design is that it looks unfinished and broken-backed when the roof panel is removed. Although the 914 looks better with the lid on, it would have looked better still if the roof had been painted to match the body. The most successful 914 variants were equipped with flared wheel-arches and a very aggressive front end, which made them look like racers – where everyone expects function to take precedence over elegance.

Back Home Again
2 C 914
INDIANA
D

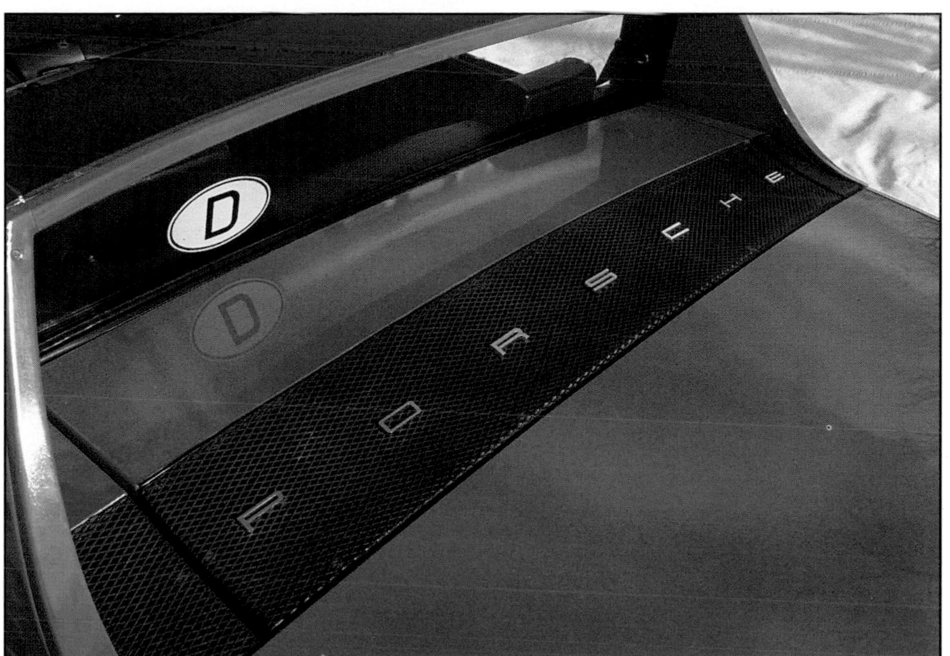
D
D
PORSCHE

From any other manufacturer, the 924 might have been judged on its own merits, and seen as a fast, reliable, comfortable and surprisingly economical car. But Porsche is not just any manufacturer, and people expected more comfort, more smoothness, more performance and more individuality. As a result, the 924 is a surprisingly affordable car on the used market today. This one dates from 1977, a couple of years after the original introduction, and the year that the 5-speed gearbox replaced the 4-speed.

By many objective measures, the 924 is a better car than the 911: better front/rear balance, better visibility, more room inside. Its performance also compares favorably with the earlier 911 models. And against, say, a Toyota or a Lexus, it is more distinctively and originally styled. It lacks two things, though, when you stand it next to a 911. One is that "carved from the solid" feeling which characterizes the 911, and the other is an indefinable magic. The 924 is a very nice car. The 911 is, quite simply, a 911.

PORSCHE

924

This 911SC dates from 1980, some sixteen years after the 911 first entered production. There had been many, many changes: more power, wider wheels, a more rounded body, shock-absorber bumpers...

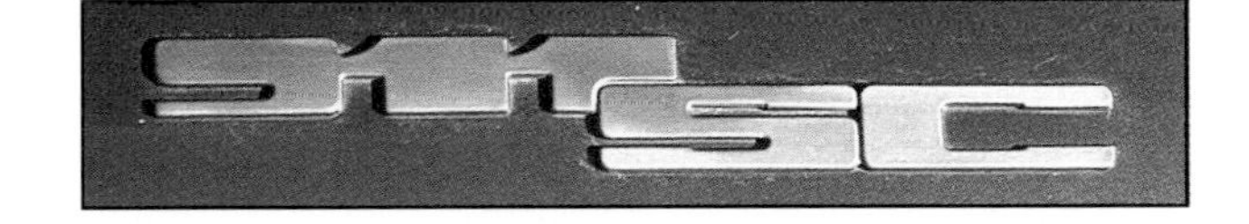

Compare the interior of this car with the interior of the 356/2 on pages 18 to 21. The seats, the trim, the instrumentation – everything is so much more comprehensive and luxurious. The trouble is that added luxury means added weight, so in order to keep the power-to-weight ratio reasonable, you need still more power.

TURBO
2M5351
INDIANA

PORSCHE

Turbocharging the 924 transformed it; the first 924 Turbos appeared in 1979, and this car dates from 1980. With 170 bhp in Europe, and 150 bhp in the United States, performance improved dramatically. Even so, the 924 Turbo was still not entirely suitable for American conditions, which tend to be "drive 'em and forget 'em." The result, if the car was not maintained, was that the turbocharger cooked after about 20,000 miles. There cannot have been much inherently wrong with the car, though: apparently, it was favored by a number of racing drivers for personal transport. In non-American markets, the 924 Turbo remains very sought-after.

MARTINIPORSCHE
DUNLOP
Shell
MARTINI PORSCHE

Left: a 935T/C Martini Porsche at an endurance race, Brands Hatch. Above: the Palmer/Lammers 956 at Silverstone in 1985. Below: a 908 chases a 935 around Brands Hatch in 1980.

Above: the Wollek/Streiff 962 takes part in the Autosport 1000 km in May 1988. Below: the Bell/Bellof 956 in Rothmans livery contests the Silverstone 1000 km in 1984. Right: the Bell/Stuck 962C leads the way around a corner at the 1985 Silverstone 1000 km. Porsches have always been particularly successful in long-distance and endurance races because, unlike most racers, they are reliable as well as fast.

Rothmans
Shell
Shell
Rothmans
PORSCHE
DUNLOP
2
Rothmans
DUNLOP
PORSCHE

The V8-engined 928 first appeared in 1977; this is a 1982 model, which bucked the usual trend by being lighter than the same model as originally introduced. By 1982, Europeans could buy the 300 bhp 928S, but Americans were restricted to the 231 bhp emission-controlled model.

Somehow, the 928 (also overleaf) never provoked the same objections as the 924. The main reason was probably sheer performance: the 924 was fast, but the 928 was very fast. Also, detail revisions to the body made the car look sleeker and faster – though feelings were mixed about the headlamp treatment.

CINTURATO P7

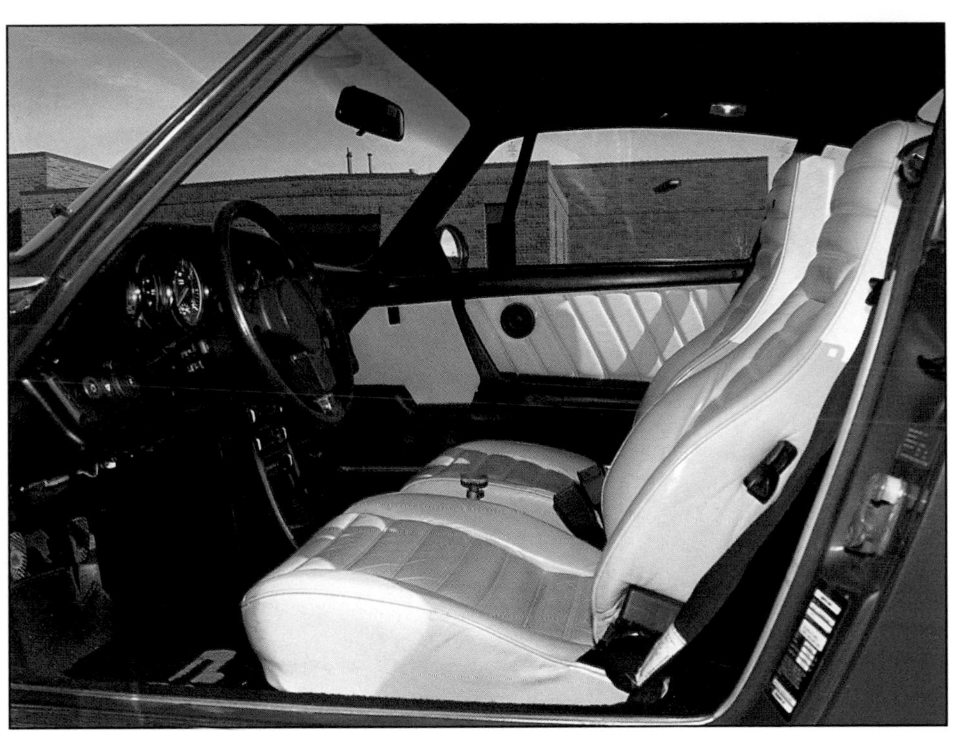

The 911 ancestry of this 1984 935 is clear: still a 911 floor pan, albeit with a high-tech composite sandwich body, and such exotic trimmings as titanium coil springs. Despite having 590 bhp from a 2856 cc turbocharged flat-six engine, and despite really needing those brake cooling slots at the front, it still looks very much like a normal car inside – a far cry from, say, Ferrari's F40.

The massive rear spoiler is doubly functional: the oil cooler lives inside it. The biggest single visual clue to the difference between a 935 and a 911 is the nose treatment, and there are kits available to make a 911 look like a 935.

PORSCHE

The 911 Turbo Sport of 1987 (also overleaf) clearly borrowed plenty of styling cues from the 935, especially the huge rear intakes and the dropped nose. Note the 6800 rpm blood line and the 180 mph speedo.

4444 KO

When this 1987 Carrera was made, the 911 had been in production for well over two decades, and the similarities between a 1964 model and this one still outweighed the differences: still a flat-six, in something very close to the original floor pan.

With the vastly increased power of the engine – swept volume had increased from 1991 cc to 3299 cc, and the maximum power of roadgoing machines had more than doubled – cooling was as much of a problem as handling. You can just see the massive oil radiator under the rear "fin" – Porsches are not air-cooled, but oil cooled! At normal road speeds, the fin is really just a glorified oil cooler, and not until well over 100 mph does it become aerodynamically very important.

PORSCHE

Carrera
PORSCHE

The glorious 959, which is also seen on pages 92 to 95, was one of the wildest road-going Porsches of all time – a modern equivalent of the old 550, and much more practical than a 935. Clearly a derivative of the 911, it is nevertheless a far cry from its parent. Four-wheel drive, with electronic traction control, would have been impressive on its own, but a Kevlar-composite body to reduce weight, and no less than 400 bhp from a turbocharged engine feeding through a six-speed gearbox, made it very potent indeed. Top speed was certainly in excess of 186 mph, though a 200 mph speedometer, instead of 220 mph, might just have been adequate. To cap all this, it was also well equipped to the point of outright luxury. The 959 was never officially "federalized" for sale in the United States.

864
Z-9278

Fitted with "bash plates" and all the other impedimenta of modern rally-driving, the 959 proved its mettle in the most demanding rally of all, the Paris-Dakar – and looked very relaxed doing it.

Rothmans
BB-PW 448
Shell
Rothmans
PORSCHE
Turbolader
SCHMITTHEIM
BOSCH
BILSTEIN

The 944S2 appeared in 1989, delivering 208 bhp from the monster four, now enlarged to just under three liters. It was the last of the 944 series, though much of its engineering lives on in the 968. Overleaf: the 924 Carrera GT, a limited edition model of 1980, predicted the shape of the 944 which appeared the following year.

CINTURATO

PIRELLI P6

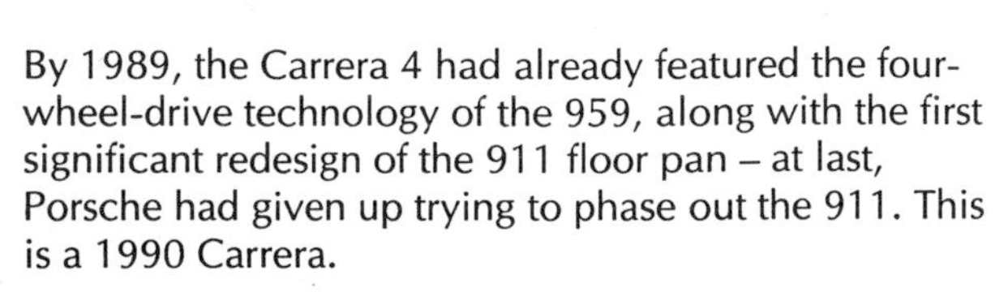

By 1989, the Carrera 4 had already featured the four-wheel-drive technology of the 959, along with the first significant redesign of the 911 floor pan – at last, Porsche had given up trying to phase out the 911. This is a 1990 Carrera.

The more it changes, the more it is the same: this 1990 Carrera looks very similar, to the casual observer, to the 911 of almost a quarter of a century before. Even the monster fixed "duck tail" is gone, restoring the purity of line.

Targa tops are all very well, but you can't beat a true convertible – Porsche prefers the term "cabriolet" – for looks or for fun. The underpinnings of the turbocharged four are shown on the opposite page, the rear transaxle improving the balance of the car and stopping it from being nose-heavy, and the view inside the engine compartment is no doubt delightful. But what must surely turn most people's heads, whether they can afford the car or not, is the wonderful combination of understated good looks and the promise of power and handling such as most manufactures cannot imagine. This is a 1990 944 S2; it is also featured overleaf.

Langeland
FORT WAYNE, IN.

PORSCHE

7147

Is the 968 a new car, or is it "only" a revamped 944? Who cares? The cabriolet in particular is surely a delightful and desirable car by any criterion. Fast, handsome, and with Porsche reliability, no-one could ask for more – unless they wanted a 928 or a 911...

PORSCHE

7289
PIRELLI

S-KX 7064